How do we understand what was, grapple with
what is and prepare for what is likely to be,
as a nation, as a people, as a community,
as individuals?

This series is an attempt to address this question
by putting into print thoughts, ideas and
concerns of some of South Asia's most seminal
thinkers.

In memory of Kozo Yamamura (1934–2017)

Learning to Live with the Past

KRISHNA KUMAR

LONDON NEW YORK CALCUTTA

'Can History Contribute to Peace?' is a revised version of a lecture delivered at the 2018 History for Peace conference 'The Idea of Culture'.

'Learning to Live with the Past' is a revised version of a lecture delivered at the 2019 conference 'Shared Histories', co-organized by History for Peace and Saint Kabir Public School, Chandigarh.

Seagull Books, 2023

© Krishna Kumar, 2023

First published in volume form
by Seagull Books, 2023

ISBN 978 1 80309 285 0

British Library Cataloguing-in-Publication Data

A catalogue record for this book
is available from the British Library

Typeset by Seagull Books, Calcutta, India
Printed and bound by WordsWorth India,
New Delhi, India

CONTENTS

CAN HISTORY CONTRIBUTE TO PEACE?

'Can history contribute to peace?' is part of the larger question: Can education contribute to peace? The record is not particularly clear. Some of the most educated countries in the world have been responsible for some of the most brutal experiences of the twentieth century, and even in South Asia, the first country to implement a universal education system, Sri Lanka, became the site of severe civil strife. And if you look at the world at large, the most aggressive country in the world, which does not shy away from intervening anywhere with messages of democracy and bombs to back them, is widely believed to have the world's most advanced system of education. Education, then, in a generic sense, cannot necessarily promise peace.

A number of philosophers have drawn the distinction between education as an idea and as a system. And though the idea or concept of education holds promise for humanity, it must wait for historical circumstances to manifest in a system. Looking for this idea in a historical vacuum is somewhat silly. To seek some clarity on this question, we can turn to a chain of peace thinkers from the twentieth century, including Jiddu Krishnamurti, Bertrand Russell and Maria Montessori.

To clarify, when I pose the question 'Can history contribute to peace?', I am referring specifically to the history taught in schools and colleges. Can this history play a role in promoting peace? This is the provocative, stimulating and promising question we will explore before returning to the broader question of whether education as a whole can promote peace. Our historical education begins during childhood and has far-reaching consequences for the individual as well as for the collective life of the society, nation and humanity. As we consider the role of history in education, it is crucial to situate ourselves in the modern world, which is unique compared to any previous era. In this world, education is an idea that has almost achieved universality. We expect education to be inclusive and fully universalized, an idea that holds unprecedented value. However, we do not know how this expansion will affect knowledge, whether it will create shared understandings or become a mechanism for regimenting the mind with certain common parameters. Unfortunately, the history of education does not provide answers to these questions in any part of the world.

The experience of expanded education systems is relatively new, especially in South Asia. In India, this idea is so new that the right to education is still being contested in court, and the Right to Education Act has already been amended twice. India's discomfort with this idea is quite evident. Sri Lanka is the only country that has some experience with universal education, yet it has struggled to cope with the consequences of an elementary-level education system. Therefore, we are venturing into uncharted territory. This is a complex undertaking because, in the modern era, education expands under the auspices of the state, making the processes of acculturation or socialization extremely intricate. Socialization, in particular, is a highly specialized term in educational theory. Peter Berger and Thomas Luckmann's seminal book, *The Social Construction of Reality*, reminds us that socialization is not a unitary process, nor does it occur uniformly throughout childhood. They have broadly categorized socialization into two phases: (i) an emotionally intense period of primary socialization, and (ii) the subsequent phase where schools come into play—secondary socialization. Primary socialization, the foundation of various studies in psychology and social anthropology, covers the first three to four years of life, critical years during which children are imprinted with essential beliefs, attitudes and anchors of the mind. The child is not yet capable of questioning and is still situated within the family at home. Can secondary socialization have an impact on primary socialization? Can schools teach children to question what they have learned and internalized before reaching school-going age? This question remains unanswered by research and warrants introspection, especially concerning history, because history, as a discipline, does not fully acknowledge how children learn.

Advances in the field of cognitive science and psychology in the twentieth century have not quite influenced the teaching of history. It seems to many that the age at which history is taught in schools may not be appropriate for children to fully engage with the subject. According to the philosopher John Dewey, whose work predates that of Jean Piaget and Lev Vygotsky, a more mature mind is perhaps required to learn history. But what is a mature mind? Dewey recommended introducing history at around the ages of 14–16, the time at which the normative achievement of some of the skills required for engaging with history might be expected. Furthermore, the development of the sense of time in children is slower than that of space and perspective. Therefore, introducing historical figures and events to young children may not achieve much at very young ages. But history as a discipline is organized with its own academic rationalism, its own history, and it leaves very little room for the school-curriculum designer or teachers.

The development of self-identity is a complex and paradoxical process, as it involves both the individual and the collective. Primary socialization already sows the roots of the collective self, those 'compulsory' forms of identity which one recognizes in retrospect in one's adolescence—that I already am, before I know who I am, a Hindu or a Muslim or a Brahmin or a Dalit. Primary socialization thus permits very little resistance against collective identity. The school curriculum then builds on this foundation and offers a collective identity broader than caste, religion and language—the national identity. The use of social sciences in education is a conscious effort to create loyal citizens who are proud of their nation. This is especially true in modern nation-states, where the state takes charge of education and uses it as a tool for acculturation and socialization. However, the development of a mature and reflective mind is necessary for a critical engagement with history and the formation of individual identity.

In 1999, I had an almost epiphanic experience while crossing the Wagah Border by bus. By then, I had familiarized myself with history textbooks from India and Pakistan, selecting a fair sample that I believed was representative of their diversity. I felt that I was aware of the broad differences between the two countries. I was headed to meet children, teachers and historians in Pakistan, intending to do the same in India upon my return. However, as our bus crossed the border, after extensive checks, I noticed a small group of boys playing cricket on the right side of the road that leads to Lahore. It struck me that these boys had a different understanding of the past than what I carried from my childhood or even the boys I knew in

Delhi. The sight of those boys playing cricket prompted me to consider what they might or might not know about something I already knew. Suddenly, I felt a significant inadequacy or unpreparedness on my part for this project. I thought I should have opted for an anthropological approach rather than an a pedagogical one, given that we were dealing with nothing less than a different culture. As Indians, we tend to view it as comparable. We emphasize cultural similarities, having suffered together during Partition. However, I felt as if I were in a foreign country and needed to understand how those boys thought. I realized that I had to start from scratch, but where was scratch? Was it 1947? 1971? Where were we, then, in 1999?

It is important to note that there is no uniform experience or understanding of history for all children. Different children read different textbooks, are taught by different teachers, attend different schools and come from different regions. These are all important factors that shape their understanding of history. Therefore, the textbook itself is just one artefact among many that shape the experience of learning history. In my research, my goal has been to find what I call the 'master narratives' of India and Pakistan. To achieve this, it is essential to consider questions such as where and how textbooks would be used, who wrote them and under what circumstances they were written.

I also wanted to explore what I refer to as 'memory posters', which are visual representations that people use to hold onto memories from their childhood or early youth. Using these two devices, I examined the 90-year period from 1857 to 1947. It's clear that both of these master narratives are moving towards the goal of freedom, which eventually resulted in Partition. As such, they are teleological in nature. However, between 1857 and approximately 1929, these narratives are almost reconcilable, and you can even see similarities among the people who populate them. It's quite gratifying to discover that this period of the past was not as divided or mutually incompatible as one might assume. However, as we approach 1930 and the final 17 years leading up to freedom and Partition, the narrative picks up speed and becomes irreconcilably divergent. It is no longer possible to see parallels between the two, and they move in different directions. One narrative celebrates the freedom from colonial rule but also mourns the tragedy of Partition, while the other narrative finds happiness in the separation and places less emphasis on the freedom achieved as a result. Conveying these two emotions is very challenging.

During my research, I had the opportunity to meet numerous Pakistani teachers and students, particularly several girls at Lahore Grammar School. These encounters left me with poignant memories of how they approached the subject of Partition. I often reflect on the things they said, such as *Why did we leave you in 1947?* and *Why, 70 years later, do we still have little evidence that it was worth it?* This sentiment is expressed repeatedly, sometimes as a subtext and sometimes more explicitly, but it is a powerful emotion. By delving deeper into the subtext and utilizing advanced techniques for uncovering meaning, the Pakistani historical narrative can be distilled into a narrative of justification. This justification includes a sense of guilt but also the belief that the guilt is worth bearing because 'the cause was worth it!' In contrast, the Indian narrative is not a *why* narrative, but rather a *how* and *who* narrative. It focuses on how the project was lost and who was responsible for it. This is how the Indian narrative navigates the last three years from 1944 to 1947, repeatedly questioning how things went so wrong. While freedom was ultimately achieved, the Indian narrative grapples with how Partition occurred.

We are left with two contrasting projects for socializing the youth. The first is a secular agenda that aims to instil a sense of modern Indian identity, emphasizing the diversity of the country and the importance of respecting it. This narrative regards the 'other' as non-secular and feels a strong sense of discomfort about this fact. The 'other' is seen as deeply religious and, as accepted by the history academia, communal (known as *saampradaayik* in Hindi). According to this narrative, Pakistan's creation is an illegitimate result of the nationalist struggle. When Pakistan hardened further, especially after 1971, its nation-building project and identity agenda moved westwards towards becoming an Islamic state. Its children were socialized through Pakistan Studies, which is no longer history but a tool for nation-building. The enfeebled and divided Pakistan of 1971 paved the way for the new incompatibility with the Indian project of socializing children to believe that India is morally more accommodative and, therefore, has justifiable superiority as a modern nation compared to its neighbour, whose nation-building project was communal from the outset and became even more so after 1971.

From the Pakistani side, the incompatibility with the Indian project is no less significant. Pakistan's agenda of socializing its youth is founded on the idea that India's self-image is a myth and need not be taken too seriously. Pakistan believes India to be hypocritical and projecting a secular identity that will inevitably be exposed as false. This ominous message continues to reverberate throughout South Asia and is becoming louder as we approach 2024.

This issue between India and Pakistan is not limited to history classrooms. In fact, Partition and Independence are typically the last chapters of history taught in schools. History essentially stops at 1947 and political science takes over from there. However, this hostile relationship between neighbours has a profound impact on the culture of our schools, classrooms and media, including cinema, television and even parliament and its televised proceedings. The noise of life permeates education, encompassing excellent actors who perform love, friendship and also terrible, bloody enmity, memorable wars, including large, smaller and experimental ones fought with Pakistan. Consequently, militaristic memory building is continuously underway around the universalized system of education that aims to educate everyone, contributing to modern nation-building. Education does not function in isolation, and it is a significant aspect of the broader reality, which we tend to overlook. This cliché often causes us to forget that education is a critical component of nation-building. The idea of universalizing education for citizenship education needs to be viewed beyond the textbook or curriculum or teaching methodologies. All questions of quality must be contextualized within the ethos of the educational institutions, including private ones.

The functioning of schools as a modern institution involves the essential device of regimentation of the child's body, mind and heart, which is used to reach the educational goals of the state. Studies conducted in India and around the world have shown that compliance is a necessary skill for every child to learn, which starts from the nursery years. The compliance of the body, which French sociologist Pierre Bourdieu describes as 'habitus', is an important aspect of this culture that includes body language, behaviour and thoughts. In order to become a successful student, a child must internalize and take on this enveloping culture. The ability to make a group of 30 or 40 children work together is essential for any school education to function, and if you are a schoolteacher, you understand its importance. Although the word *regimentation* is commonly associated with the military or police, its use in schools is equally interesting and compelling. Therefore, it is essential to understand how schools function as a process and institution. It is important to note that this regimentation occurs not only in public schools but also in private ones.

I understand that in order to ensure effective functioning of schools, certain forms of 'habitus' creation are necessary, particularly when the classroom is diverse. I am presenting these points for analysis purposes and not for criticism. As one goes up the hierarchy of schools, one notices that they distinguish themselves in terms of their effectiveness and quality by using another word that is almost a cousin of regimentation— *discipline*. The higher the status of the school in the market, the more they depend on their ability to claim that their children are disciplined and can be relied upon to behave in certain ways. By the time students finish school, the school's stamp is so deeply imprinted that they carry it with them for the rest of their lives, and they identify themselves by saying 'I am from such-and-such school!' They can even spot another person from their school in a crowd without having to ask. This is what Bourdieu referred to as 'habitus'—institutional memories that manifest not just in our language but also in our bodies.

In addition to compliance and discipline, another important regimenting device that is often ignored in schools (you might use the term *elite* for those schools that use it more successfully and purposefully) is the ability to answer questions quickly without thinking. Unthinking quickness is an aspect of regimentation that 'good' schools inculcate, which helps students become increasingly competitive. In ninth-grade classrooms in famous schools in Calcutta or Delhi, for example, the teacher may not even finish the question before students start raising their hands. This unthinking quickness and the desire to answer before anyone else is a consequence of long-standing socialization values that do not quite match the expectation of critical inquiry, which requires reflection and taking a few seconds or minutes before answering a question. That is something that regimentation cannot create. Answers are given on the assumption that the question does not require thought—it only requires recall. This leads to the fourth source of regimentation: fear of examinations, where so much needs to be recalled under great pressure that preparation, from nursery to the next 13–14 years, may prove inadequate.

Hence, the use of fear as a tool for regimentation is prevalent in schools, causing students to live in a constant state of anxiety and adopt a rote learning approach for exams. Drill and coaching classes are seen as supplements to school education, especially in higher grades. As a history teacher, one must be cognizant of these factors when using history as a means to foster critical thinking. In an environment where regimentation is deeply ingrained, socializing the mind into critical enquiry through the study of history can be challenging. During my research on Indo-Pak history, I spoke with history teachers in both countries who acknowledged their lack of control over such aspects of school life. In the lower grades, history teachers may not even have a background in history. It is only in higher classes that history becomes an optional subject and a qualified history teacher can be guaranteed. Therefore, the question of whether teaching history alone can promote reflexivity and open-mindedness in a culture of regimentation requires careful consideration of the many difficulties involved.

One major aspect that history contributes to nation-building is the creation of a national narrative in the modern world. At the school level, all history narratives are essentially national narratives that describe how events unfolded within the nation's territory. However, it is important to approach the nation-building project without excessive sensitivity, as the nationalist project has been hijacked and vitiated by the current political circumstances in India. The situation was similar in Pakistan 70 years ago. In this context, it is worth considering whether nation-building can be achieved without political nationalism or whether it is possible to engage with political nationalism in creative ways. Can we aspire to be Indians without being nationalists, as Rabindranath Tagore dreamed? This is a challenging question that requires careful consideration.

Moving forward, we must consider the present-day concern regarding school textbooks and the National Council of Educational Research and Training (NCERT). It is noteworthy that the very first word of the acronym NCERT is 'national'. The creation of new textbooks for different subjects, including history, in 2006, 2007 and 2008 has been well received, particularly among those of us who are involved in English-medium schools and who could be considered part of a national elite. As someone who was a part of the NCERT during those fortuitous years, I feel especially gratified. The success story of these textbooks makes us believe that we can make a positive impact through education.

As we delve into broader questions on peace and education's role in promoting peace worldwide, I would like to recount a particular story. India and Pakistan are both incredibly diverse countries. Although India's diversity cannot be encapsulated in a museum, the National Crafts Museum in Delhi's vicinity provides a glimpse into that diversity, unlike the National Museum. To truly appreciate its extent, one must visit state museums like the Bihar Museum in Patna or the museums in Tamil Nadu or elsewhere. Similarly, in Pakistan, the Lok Virsa Museum, located approximately 20 kilometers from Islamabad, is a museum dedicated to the women of Pakistan. In the first gallery, you will encounter the Vedas, the Buddha, and various other layers of identity that the museum claims Pakistan has inherited. As you explore the various galleries of this remarkable museum, which takes almost a whole day, you can celebrate and recognize the extent to which Pakistan has embraced its internal diversity.

The issue of school textbooks becomes even more significant when we consider the high levels of diversity in both India and Pakistan. These countries are hierarchically organized societies, with highly unequal education systems. The NCERT produces trans-provincial textbooks that cover approximately 10 per cent of schools in India, with this percentage having increased since the National Curriculum Framework 2005 was introduced. However, it is important to recognize that this 10 per cent primarily comprises private schools that follow the Central Board of Secondary Education (CBSE) curriculum, with only a limited coverage of India's secondary education system. The overwhelming majority of Indians attend provincial schools that cater mostly to the lower strata of society, and it is here where education becomes mass education. By using NCERT textbooks, which are primarily available in English (and also Hindi and Urdu), we overlook the challenges faced by provincial India.

The NCERT still sends experts to many occasions, but its textbooks have not impressed any major publisher in India, nor the ICSE school system, which has not bothered to look at either the curriculum or syllabus on which NCERT books are based. When people look at these textbooks, they feel proud and happy, but they fail to recognize the financial and academic investment required to create them. How was it possible to do so during the first UPA government, and can other countries, such as Pakistan or Sri Lanka, achieve similar results with the books that we sometimes belittle and make fun of? These are deep questions that require examination.

The history of history textbook making in NCERT is worth recalling. In 1967, Professor Romila Thapar wrote the Class 6 and 7 textbooks of history. These were the first textbooks of their kind, and if you look at her opening chapter, you will be struck by its imagination. In fact, that opening chapter could be reproduced today in one of these 2006, 2007, 2008 books and it would look quite fitting. She spoke about the past as an archaeological find where you find a clay pitcher, not the whole pitcher but just a piece, and with its help, you had to piece together an idea of what that clay pitcher might have looked like, who might have used it and what kind of society might have existed whose people were using it. She introduced the question of sources, used the idea of historical imagination, and so on. In 1967! Had that book never been written, or had she not engaged with textbook development as a senior academic at that time, the 2006 books would not have been possible. These textbooks dilute the regimenting agenda of schools, make history come alive, and create the possibility of critical inquiry, making them the hallmark of history teaching.

These books became possible because we had been there and lived through a 30-year-old or a 40-year-old controversy over history books. We saw shifts in various parts of the country, but not necessarily because of a shift of government. This is a much more complex story than people would like to acknowledge. If we acknowledge that story and accept that we are lucky to have something which can be used for promoting critical enquiry, why is that not happening? We merely curse the teachers—they are the spoil-sports, they don't know how to use these books, we have done our job, but they can't do theirs—'Can't they understand what it means to be imaginative?' and so on.

It is important to consider who becomes a teacher, their working conditions, and more significantly, who studies in the schools. Who studies the NCERT textbooks and who studies the Uttar Pradesh state-board or Gujarat state-board textbooks? When making comparisons between textbooks, it is essential to compare the Gujarat textbook to the Sri Lankan textbook, rather than the NCERT textbook, for it to be a valid comparison.

Pakistan's federal curriculum wing has limited resources and academic access to work. When I visited, a military officer was in charge, and his job was to coordinate and send orders. No country in the world has an institution like the NCERT, modelled on the Central Pedagogiska Institute of Moscow, which is a relic of the Nehruvian era. We must congratulate ourselves as a nation for having a democratically acting institution like NCERT that promotes participatory democracy.

We should not lose this narrative because of our dislike for it, especially now when 'nationalism' and 'nation-building' have become tools of manipulation. Participatory democracy, which the National Curriculum Framework tries to promote, comprises critical citizens and historians who do not criticize their South Asian neighbours because they are poorer and do not have the resources or knowledge to invest in this subject. Even our own states do not know what to do about it.

Can history contribute to peace? It can. Can education contribute to peace? It can. However, to turn this *can*, this possibility, into reality, we will have to answer the more crucial question of what we mean by *peace*.

Education involves the creation of a shared language, a universe of discourse, through the use of words. If education is successful, words alone should suffice to run societies, manage the world and deal with dissent and hostility. However, achieving this goal is a complex endeavour that requires a deep understanding of education itself.

To be effective, education must take place in real classrooms, guided by dedicated teachers responsible for each child's learning. Only then can we responsibly assess whether education can contribute to peace. In today's world of social media and rapid communication technologies, this task has become even more challenging. Can we use words in a way that they are not distorted by the time they reach their intended audience? Can our words remain intact, or will the listener or reader impose their own meanings onto them? While it is the right of the listener or reader to interpret words in their own way, the creation of a shared universe of discourse requires careful preparation, and schools have a responsibility to impart this knowledge.

In building this shared language, societies must work with teachers, who represent the education agenda and are entrusted to implement the syllabus. Textbooks are only as good as the syllabus, and the syllabus is only as good as the curriculum, which are distinct categories of educational theory that are often overlooked. A textbook is merely an artefact that does not reveal the architectural plan of the curriculum or the details of the fittings that the syllabus presents, much like fittings in a house that the architecture creates.

If we expect history to contribute to peace, the teaching of history must prioritize cultivating curiosity about the past and respect for the artefacts, monuments and ruins that have been left for us to study. Without curiosity and respect, we risk losing these valuable remnants to the destructive actions of vandals.

We should strive to view the past as a source of fascination and exploration, and impart tools for historical research that allow every child to participate in the excitement of piecing together the jigsaw puzzle of events that occurred long ago.

To achieve this goal, historians must engage more deeply with other educators and stakeholders involved in school education. They must work closely with psychologists, social anthropologists, history teachers, and school principals to create a curriculum that fosters curiosity, exploration and critical thinking. This engagement really does involve a bit of an additional activity in our system—the most meaningful activities in our system are known as extra-curricular activities!

LEARNING TO LIVE WITH THE PAST

How do we arrive at the choice to live *with* the past and recognize that the past is past? That not much can be done about it? This, as opposed to living *in* the past—thinking that the past was better and not just different, thinking that the past gives us a sense of a goal to achieve or feeling nostalgic about its passage, and so on. This subject acquires a great deal of potency when the past is represented by the Partition of the Indian subcontinent in 1947. The idea of the Partition continues to be a matter of passion and nostalgia, depending on which side of the border you are on. One is thinking not just about the physical border—the Wagah border—but also the borders within. If you are a secular-minded, progressive person, who believes that India's national destiny was and is different from that of Pakistan, then you feel the Partition was not just wrong but in fact a failure. The Partition means everything that we reject as progressive Indians, following those we regard as leaders: Gandhi, Nehru and various others. On the other side are people who think of the Partition border as a reminder of a betrayal, a conspiracy. They too would like to undo Partition, but for very different reasons. From a secular perspective, we call them communal people—people who would like to re-create an undivided India but name it differently, call it *Akhand Bharat*.

Partition evokes a significant sense of separation: ideological separations within our country, and a separation from what society (and the country) was perceived to be. From that point of view, the Partition is certainly a very challenging problem for the history teacher. But then, it's not just the Partition that is challenging. Think of the average history teacher, who has a clearly cut-out job to do—a syllabus to complete, a prescribed textbook to follow, children to be prepared for examination based on that textbook. Within such a system, it can be a major challenge if the teacher is imaginative and wants to make history come alive. If she doesn't belong in this category, then she will not teach history in the sense of history-as-subject. This latter teaching method arouses our curiosity about the past, tells us something about it, hopes to make us interested in where we come from and how the world got to where it is today. If one is the kind of teacher who simply completes the syllabus and leaves the subject cold, we can't critique it except by saying that she is a teacher doing a job.

But think about the imaginative teacher. Quite often she can be in a complicated, uncharted space. If the past becomes too alive, leaving little epistemic space between where the students are, where we are positioned today, and where the past was, then we might lose track of its 'pastness'. One true thing about the past is that it was drastically different from our present. History that is well taught ought to make us aware of this complete difference. As philosophers say, the past is like a foreign country. When you enter the past, you are looking at a different world, a different landscape. The good teacher can bring us close to this past by using pedagogically progressive methods.

Our empathy with those who lived in the past (especially prominent personalities), combined with the various pedagogic techniques that make the past 'come alive', can result in a bit of an injustice to what history teaching can and should be able to achieve in the curriculum. It's a dilemma, a paradox. Should we make history come alive? If so, then how do we prevent it from creating the desire to undo that past? That's exactly the kind of question which arises when you think about the Partition.

Seven decades on, we haven't reconciled with the Partition—neither we, as thoughtful critical Indians, nor the people across the border. They still think that Partition didn't do enough justice to them. So, here is an episode of history which has a bit of a problem when brought alive—what an imaginative teacher can do through visuals, theatre, biographies, live storytelling and other methods available in the pedagogic kitty. This problem is not easy to depict.

It was about 22 years ago that I decided to study how history is taught in India and Pakistan. My idea was to look at the textbooks used in different parts of the two countries. I also decided to meet teachers and students on both sides, spend some time with them, and ask them to write about the Partition. This became quite a difficult and complex journey for me in terms of understanding my own field—education—and I began to realize how important the subject of history is in the curriculum. And also how difficult. No other subject can be used and abused the way history can.

But let's briefly take stock of what history is doing in the curriculum, and this goes beyond India and Pakistan. What history does in most countries is participate in the project called nation building. History is one of those three or four subjects that we used to call social studies; nowadays, we like to call them social sciences. Generally, it starts being taught in Grade 6, through to Grade 8, by which time you get an exposure to India's history as a continuous story from the ancient to the modern times. Those modern times end in Partition or Independence. After that there is no history. Then history starts again in Grade 9, and through Grade 10, one gets another chance to place Indian history that one has learnt in 6 to 8 in a wider global context. Then of course there is history in Grades 11 and 12 for those who want to pursue history as an optional subject, to explore the subject in some depth to make sense of things. But history at the earlier stages is part of what you would call citizenship education. History is in the curricular policies of various nation-states because it seems to satisfy the need for creating a national identity. It answers those questions which every child is expected to raise at some point or another: Who am I? Where do I belong? Where did I come from? Where did the people that I consider my people come from?

These questions are assumed to be part of one's general curiosity. It is also assumed that it's the responsibility of the school system to respond to these questions; to create answers that appear to be valid, answers that have been state-certified. The modern school, thus, is an institution of the state and draws its legitimacy from the state. As a system, it aspires to reach out to every child. It is a unique institutional creation of our times—what we call modern history. There was no such institution at any other time in the past: in our case before the present few decades, and in most countries of the world before the late nineteenth century. In all earlier periods of human history, knowledge was available in small amounts to vast numbers of people, and only a select few had the opportunity to study it in-depth. The modern school replaced this older system of distribution of knowledge, compelling one to attend school for a certain number of years, with the school working under the auspices of a state-organized system. Whether it's a state school or not, the state has a say in what the school does. This is where the curriculum comes in.

The curriculum sets our goals and objectives, which is generally the policy of the state about what education is for. What different subjects are meant for and how much space they occupy in the curriculum are all aspects of this broader policy framework. Then, of course, there is the syllabus. Most teachers think the syllabus is really the curriculum, because it's the syllabus that they have to complete (otherwise everybody seems to be angry with them). And finally, the most important of these three objects— namely, the textbook. In fact, you meet a lot of teachers who have never seen either the curriculum document or the syllabus but have seen the textbook. They know that it's the textbook that matters;

it is also what absorbs most of the anger a lot of people feel about education. It's the textbook which is important for getting qualifications through an examination process—all questions are based on the textbook. Sometimes you don't worry about the textbook if you have a guidebook, because the guidebook is a further distillation of the knowledge the textbook is supposed to provide. Guidebooks make it even more convenient for you to go straight to the relevant knowledge for passing examinations.

So the wise and practical teacher knows that their job is cut out: simply to get children through examinations by teaching the answers that are certified to be right. These 'right' answers fall in line with what the nation-state determines to be the line of thinking that citizens must possess in order to be loyal citizens. This brings us to the questions: How are political rivalries to be understood in terms of the goals of education? How does education shape political rivalry or hostility? How does the neighbourly antagonism between India and Pakistan mould the education systems of these two countries?

Education participates in this process in both subtle and not-so-subtle ways. One gets this instantly when one listens to a teacher teaching Indian history of the period, say, from the 1920–1930s onwards; there is a sense of the inevitability of the Partition. My analysis of how textbooks do this is elaborately analysed in my books *Prejudice and Pride* (2001) and *Battle for Peace* (2007). In brief, both these countries present a narrative of the freedom struggle, the struggle against colonial rulers, in a way that leads to a particular end. This end, namely, the Partition and Independence, has two different meanings for these two countries. For India, Partition was a tragic loss at a moment of great achievement. Many poets have written about that moment as a moment of light that also carried some kind of grim darkness. Other poets have tried to show us that our freedom was achieved at a great cost—the Partition—which brought with it human tragedy and loss, a sense of bitterness. That moment brought out passions that nobody thought human beings could have. In the Indian case, the narrative of history that is taught first in Grade 8, then Grade 10, and finally in Grade 12, follows this notion: yes, Independence was a great achievement; yet had it happened without the Partition, it would have been a greater achievement—we cannot forget or move on from this tragic loss. If you are an Indian studying the history of the freedom struggle, then you cannot help but think of the Partition as something very sad.

In Pakistan, the Partition has a very different meaning. It carries the idea that it was a moment of birth—the birth of a country from which its history as a modern nation begins. Pakistani historiography often sees the seeds of Partition in the distant past. Depending on how much influence the Islamization policies that gripped Pakistan from 1970s onward had on one, they will place the seeds of Partition far out in the distance. There are those who believe these seeds were sown in the 1930s; others, in late nineteenth century; and still others who think that those seeds existed in the tenth century, Pakistan being the fruition of a very long struggle. The Pakistani narrative posits the Partition as a bit of an escape: claiming that had the Pakistani leaders not been persistent, Pakistanis might have missed the Partition and they might still be under the Hindu Raj—what Pakistani textbooks like to call the dominant forces at the time of India's Independence.

The two narratives are different not just in the conception of the ending. They are different in what they mention where, how much space they give to these mentions, what they are silent about, which decades and periods they highlight, and also in how they pace the narrative. It's not as if they are complete mirror images; instead they are contrary in a nuanced way. They locate the beginning of the freedom struggle in the same year (by Grade 8, you know that moment was 1857)—the one common thing about history learning in both countries. Up till about the 1920s, the two narratives are not very different. But this changes once great personalities enter the narratives. What is history without personalities? It's the personalities who lend visuals to history. In the case of India, that personality is Mahatma Gandhi. In the case of Pakistan, Muhammad Ali Jinnah—and before him, Muhammad Iqbal.

The taught histories of the two countries also choose specific periods in the lives of these personalities. For example, in the case of Iqbal, the Indian and Pakistani school history textbook writers seem to divide his life into two parts: before and after 1930. Indian history writers prefer the earlier Iqbal while their Pakistani counterparts prefer the later Iqbal. Before Iqbal gave his speech at the All-India Muslim League's annual session in Allahabad in December 1930, proposing the 'two-nation theory', he was believed to be a different kind of person, even though he remained a poet to the end. It's the post-1930 Iqbal that interests people across the border where he is regarded as a key figure responsible for the birth of Pakistan. One can go into numerous details about how these two versions of history differ. Such as, why the Pakistani version emphasizes the Nehru Report of 1928, which demanded dominion status for India from the British rulers and reservation of seats for minorities in legislatures, while in India it is not all that important. Similarly, the developments of the late 1930s in the freedom struggle are far more significant from a Pakistani point of view. The

1940s are covered in two distinct and different paces in these two sets of textbooks: the Indian textbooks move speedily through that period whereas the Pakistani ones move very slowly, dwelling on each event that helped the Muslim League proceed towards the goal of creating a new nation. Pakistani textbooks generate a sense of the destiny of their nation.

This very brief summary of what I found should suffice to indicate how important the nation-building role of history teaching is in both countries. That role can actually be pinned down to the creation of a civic commitment to the nation-state. It's not surprising that history is backed with larger training in the discipline of civics. Civics, in fact, is still called 'civics' in most schools, even though in India we have tried to rename it 'social and political life learning'. But the term civics continues to be used, and it has a very close relationship with history in how it brings us to the moment when certain values of the nation are born. History bears witness to the rise of those values by showing that their seeds lie in the past. So if the values are those of the Constitution of India, then the freedom struggle becomes the period in history during which those values came to the fore. The Indian historical narrative underplays the differences among movements, leaders and factions within the freedom struggle. It also underpins the dissenting views about what the future nation would be.

The idea that history ought to play an inspirational role is fundamental to how history finds its status and place in the curriculum. This is true in all countries of the world; India and Pakistan are no exceptions. We would like our children to realize that the Constitution came out of a historical struggle, and the qualities that the Constitution is supposed to represent arose through the debates and battles of the various political leaders of that struggle. In the case of Pakistan, where the Constitution continues to be a matter of political struggle to this day, the idea of an Islamic identity stands in the place of history. This has led to the creation of the idea that Pakistan's destiny as a Muslim nation was written in its past and has come to fruition today. So the idea of citizenship building is the civic awareness that Pakistan is an Islamic state, that the values of Islam are the values of Pakistan, and that's what history is supposed to teach the nation's children. Thus, in both cases, the inclusion of history in the curriculum essentially serves a moral purpose—to create a sense of pride in the nation and its past. This purpose easily lends itself to the creation of an identity, a collective identity that gives us a sense of a collective self. And this is where the most important mutation of emotions takes place.

The growth of a collective identity is facilitated when it has the 'other' to seek inspiration from. It becomes easier to define who we are if we can say we are different, different from the other, especially when this other happens to be close by, which makes the task even more convenient. We are what they are not—this notion of a collective identity as a curricular responsibility falls most heavily on the shoulders of the history teacher. It's the history teacher who is responsible for creating pride in ourselves and prejudice towards the other. Prejudice is perhaps the wrong word; rather, the job is helping us recognize what the other is or is not. The Partition is the kind of subject which cannot be 'properly' learnt, because history syllabi or textbooks on either side of the border will only facilitate learning that resonates with the purpose of history as defined by the respective states.

In India, the Partition is regarded as the product of a failure—in the worst possible words, you could call it a conspiracy in which Muslims and the British came together to practise what, according to so many textbooks, the British were practising: the policy of divide and rule. Many textbooks in India would like to show that the Partition sowed the seeds of a continuation of colonial dominance. If these two countries continued to war, then it was easier for Britain, the rest of Europe and the West to dominate the world order.

In Pakistan, the Partition has a very different connotation: a destiny that was finally realized despite every attempt made to resist it by people who didn't want Pakistan to be born. Now the sense of 'otherness' that this portrayal creates is quite exclusive to that other, and does not allow any room for what the past can then be—a resource for so many goals of education, one goal simply being curiosity. Not only the past but even the present loses the possibility of that goal. In India, the curiosity about how that other country is or how it shapes the lives of its people, what kind of society it is—such thoughts are completely muzzled. The last news we have of

Pakistan from our textbooks is the news of Partition, after which there is nothing—no textbook tells us about what happened thereon. Then the mouthpiece is handed over to the cinema, to the media, to gossip and lore of various kinds.

On the Pakistani side, the situation is quite similar. Curiosity about India is aroused mainly by its films which continue to be very popular in Pakistan. But as far as school-level learning is concerned, it stops with Partition. After that it's not worth learning about India; curiosity comes to a stop. But then, curiosity is not something that sits easy with education systems in either India or Pakistan. Curiosity, as we know, is a natural instinct in a child; it doesn't serve much of a purpose in learning unless it turns into inquiry. Making a child's natural curiosity sustainable over adulthood requires that tools of enquiry be imparted—and in this lies the role of the modern school. The school can turn a child's natural curiosity into this spirit of inquiry. History is eminently suited to this task. The child can learn by either knowing how to find out what the past was like or by reading history with the awareness of how history is written. But if history is presented as ready-made, as history that answers all the relevant questions, it ceases to inspire curiosity or help develop the tools of inquiry. History is not even defined in the curriculum as a subject which is meant to arouse curiosity and inquiry about the past in most states in India, and certainly not in Pakistan. In fact, it is usually considered a subject that hands us the answers to questions like: How did we get here? How did we become a modern nation?

What is it that distinguishes us as a modern nation in the world?

History is essentially a subject that involves civic learning, and therefore, the teacher who uses history to arouse some sense of inquiry about the past is a rare teacher. And if she is serious about her business, she most probably won't be able to complete her syllabus. Any study of history requires engagement with certain topics; once you engage with a topic and facilitate learning with the help of resources, distinguish real evidence from fake, and once you begin to see the teaching of history in terms of such epistemological or intellectual goals, the pace at which we organize history teaching cannot be sustained. And so a majority of teachers won't even think about it. In any case, history figures as a marginal subject in the social sciences;

with emphasis placed on more practical subjects, such as mathematics and commerce, history has been further marginalized. History is also problematic because it is taught by not only teachers and curriculum designers but also the entertainment industry which finds in history enormous fodder for its use. On every possible subject, you can find any number of appealing cinematic versions and narratives. The media conveys to children many versions of and much information about the past in ways far more attractive than what a blackboard or a smartboard can do. This makes the task of a good history teacher even more difficult.

So, how do we create a sense of the past where the possibility of learning about its wider landscape of life remains insatiable and uncertain, yet full of possibilities? There are shared pasts and conflicting histories, and the task of the judicious, capable and interested history teacher is to make the subject a means of creating interest in the past, and learning about the ways in which the past presents itself as a challenge to our intellect, to our abilities to inquire about the past. Then alone can history serve the purposes which we would consider synonymous with peace. History otherwise is a subject that lends itself very easily to political hostility, simply because of the conditions in which it is taught and because of the manner in which it is structured for inclusion in the education system. History lends itself most easily to that structure as a means of creating a sense of a continued battle with the past. Instead of learning that the past is actually past and the best it can do is to help us to become curious about it, to respect it and to create in us the capacities to live with what has already happened, history often ends up creating a sense of nostalgia. The idea that something that happened 400 years ago can now be undone or that it ought to be undone so that justice can be served is precisely the product of that kind of thinking. Or the feeling that the Partition was a mistake and should be reversed or that it was a conspiracy and therefore it should be undone is a similar case.

There is much potential in history as a subject for peace, but how little that potential is utilized. Under systemic education, that potential is not only not realized even to a marginal degree but is, in fact, subverted so that history becomes a means by which children's regimentation can proceed further. The school is a regimental institution, in the sense that it controls bodies from the time they are in kindergarten. Children learn to live in an environment in which freedom is frowned upon—any sense of freedom has to be bottled up for life outside the school. If you are a student of educational anthropology, you can stand outside any school and see how much difference it makes when children emerge from the school gate or enter the school bus. Nowadays, many schools like to put a teacher on every bus, so that the children remain in somewhat of a school environment even when they are on their way home—because, of course, the heavens will fall if the children are left to themselves! The fact that the history teacher works in an environment in which most of the subjects participate in the regimentation of the child's body and mind makes the task of the history teacher, even the imaginative history teacher, extremely challenging. If we are therefore talking about South Asia as a region that calls for a contribution to peace through education, then we have to recognize the limitations imposed on us by the system and work our way out of those limitations to the extent possible.

South Asia is divided by the borders of nation-states, each of which has its own history that privileges its collective identity. So there is a history of Pakistan, a history of Bangladesh—Pakistan's history as a modern nation begins in 1947, Bangladesh's in 1971. Sri Lanka and Nepal also have their own collective identities to which their school histories have now been fully tailored.

School history ultimately creates a sense of hard borders, and if education were a humanist enterprise, then it should dilute those borders. That's what it would mean if we paid better attention to what we call—or might call—'shared' histories or 'better' histories to create a sense of a shared past. What would that mean? To begin with, it would mean, at least in Pakistan, that India still has not accepted Pakistan. The one thing that Pakistan's history and other textbooks emphasize is that Pakistan is a very insecure society because it is next to India which still doesn't recognize it. From their perspective, India is not happy about the existence of Pakistan.

I can never forget my interaction with Grade 9 children of the Lahore Grammar School of Pakistan, in which a girl asked me: 'Why are you, despite the fact that you are such a big country, afraid of us?' Of course, my colleague and I tried our best to explain to her that we Indians were not afraid. Then she asked, 'Then why did you make that atom bomb?' I didn't cut much ice with her and the other children when I said that the atomic bomb is not necessarily for them, that in fact we have other hostile neighbours. She said, 'Well, those are there, but are you telling me that it is not for us? Are you really telling me the truth?' Now that was a very difficult question when it comes from a Grade 9 student who is quite sure that she knows the answer. This feeling of insecurity is reciprocated in better or worse ways by India. We too are insecure and, as you know from our current climate, we can exercise all our political options around the issue of security and forget about unemployment, food shortages and everything else.

Both nations are permanently insecure because of the sense of 'the other not accepting us'. Pakistan because we don't accept them; India thinks Pakistan doesn't accept what happened in Kashmir—which is also a political reality. So, if we were to deny the possibility of their version of history being taught there and say, 'Look, your history is false and our history is true,' then we will only exacerbate that sense of denial which already exists in their minds. And perhaps something very similar will happen to many people on this side of the border. In relation to Bangladesh and countries of the region too, if we denied their nation-state-centric narratives, then we won't get very far.

It seems to me that the possibility of exploring shared pasts has to be realized within the context of how history is taught in a nationalist framework. We can certainly soften that framework. If we were looking for a way to move forward, we would say 'Yes, there is a difference between a hard nationalist framework and a reasonable nationalist framework.' Nationalism in itself has many nuances and categories; therefore we need not—we cannot—dismiss the idea of the 'national' as something inspiring, as an idea that brings people together across castes and religions and communities. We don't need to sacrifice that idea just because nationalism sometimes becomes a threat to humanism, as Rabindranath Tagore has famously pointed out in his text about the dangers of political nationalism gone wild.

Without denying a national narrative that history attempts to generate in an education system meant for all children, we can still create spaces for exploring a past that is distant—a past that takes us into distances that we otherwise regard as either too far or irrelevant. This is because that longer past doesn't go away; it drips into and links to later pasts and the recent past that we hold so dearly. Learning how pasts come together, how pasts stitch together, inquiring into how those stitches work, through what channels they work, political and otherwise—it would be a very interesting exercise if we were to infuse the history curriculum with these possibilities. That is not an easy exercise given how rigid the system is, how limited the space available for any kind of social inquiry. To imagine a South Asia in which hostilities gradually calm down and the region becomes an ethical, psychological reality rather than merely a geographical entity for the map maker might seem like a fantasy, but one that can infuse some spirit into a stifling education system that leaves very little room for resistance to regimentation.

Given that this education system is a universal one through which every child has to pass, it becomes even more necessary, in a logical and fundamental sense, to infuse it with the possibilities of learning about the past in ways that are unconstrained by modern national borders—but without challenging those borders. One often hears about such experiments in some limited, elite circles. But such experiments don't have to be confined to a few children or a few teachers who encourage children to learn about how things happened differently in different parts of the past. Past is a region, a very vast region in which we can find room for our curiosity and inquiry if we are not driven by an inspirational agenda, a kind of moral agenda of history, which is the reality of our times.